Egypt

REFLECTIONS ON CONTINUITY

RICHARD PARE

TIMKEN PUBLISHERS, INC. ⊓t⊔ NEW YORK, 1990

To my parents, Phyllis and David Pare

Acknowledgements

Egypt has inspired some of the most resonant images in the history of photography. The works of such pioneers as du Camp, Greene, Teynard, de Clerq, and Frith were part of my visual knowledge of the country before I began working there. I give grateful acknowledgment to them and to my teachers for guidance and for the examples they have set.

This project would not have come about had it not been for Dr. Doris E. C. Shoukri of the American University in Cairo, who made it possible for me to stay in Egypt for an extended period. Dr. George Scanlon of the American University gave valuable advice on matters relating to Islamic architecture and suggested places in remote corners of Cairo that I otherwise would not have found. Dr. Ahmed Kadry, former chairman of the Egyptian Antiquities Organization, Cairo, granted me permission to photograph at sites under his department.

In the oasis of Farafra, I was able to work through the friendship of Mr. Badr, Mr. Ewes, and Mr. Mohammed, whose trust in my intention made me welcome in the community. They gave me a vision of life in the oasis that remains among the most treasured of my memories, one that will be always with me.

For their help in many ways I would like to thank Deborah Bell, Bokelberg, Perihan Boutros-Ghali, Eun Mo Chung, John Coplans, Lee Friedlander, Rudolf Kicken, Gregorio Marañon, Gerd Sander, Mr. and Mrs. Fouad Tahir, and Matthew Weinreb. For the design of the book I would like to thank Eleanor Morris Caponigro. The photographs were made while I was on sabbatical from the Canadian Centre for Architecture; I would like to thank Phyllis Lambert, director of the Centre, for her support.

I would like to express my profound gratitude to the people of Egypt for their goodwill and generosity of spirit, which made my passage through the country rewarding and enriching.

Frontispiece: Postcard stand, Luxor.

Egypt: Reflections on Continuity

Egypt is a thin green line that runs through the history of the civilized world. The fertile Nile valley has seen the rise and fall of civilizations since the beginning of recorded history. The great richness and diversity of Egypt speak of a continuity in the essential aspect of a society that is civilized in the deepest sense. The Egyptian people have an innate grace and vitality, and an understanding of the culture that is part of their heritage. They have emerged from centuries of foreign domination, retaining a great independence of spirit. Theirs is a country of contrasts: the desert and the verdant abundance of the cultivated land along the Nile and in the oases; the ancient remains of the past mingled with the turbulent present; the chaos of the modern city and the utter silence and space of night in the desert.

This book is a celebration of Egypt. The photographs are arranged with the flow of my memory of the country: from the river to the desert, the oases, the modern and ancient city of Cairo, and back in time to the pharaonic antiquities of the Nile valley, and then once more to the desert beyond the pyramids. To be in Egypt is to redefine the culture for oneself. It is necessary to contend with issues of change and eternity, to find the enduring through the ephemeral. What is transient, and what will continue? What part of the transient is necessary, and of that necessary part what shall be recorded? Reflection on continuity may lead to transfiguration of subject, bringing deeper insight into the familiar and recognition of the sublime.

Cairo

Cairo is intensely alive in the midst of history, with a complex overlaying of centuries constantly before one's eyes. In the middle of the modern city the great statue of Ramesses II, brought from Memphis, gazes out with calm serenity over the roar of traffic. Below the embankment alongside the Nile, the water of the great river moves unvaryingly downstream, as it has since the Aswan High Dam was built in the far south. The river stands at the heart of Egypt and symbolizes it in a way no other river is equated with a national identity. It is because of the Nile that Egypt exists.

At the boundary of ancient Cairo, the city's character becomes medieval. The mingling of old and new compounds an awareness of the accretion of time. People stand opposite the gate built by Saladin at the time of the Crusades, selling great mounds of produce. In the narrow streets of the old city, the traffic moves at the pace of a man on foot, past the shadowed glories of previous centuries.

The university of al-Azhar in the old city has been a center of learning for more than a thousand years; here students still ascend to the roof to read. Looking out, they can contemplate the skyline articulated by richly decorated minarets of innumerable mosques, the legacy of Islam, built when the city was incalculably wealthy and filled with the goods of the world passing between continents.

The desert between Kharga and Dakhla oasis.

The road across the desert is unrelieved in its monotony if the traveler passes too quickly. The differentiation of surface is subtle, and it is necessary to walk out across the desert floor to distinguish variations in the essentially level ground. The bottom of what was once an ocean is scattered with seashells. Fossil corals still stand where they lived in another geological era. Threads of quartz mark off the ground in linear divisions. Complex star-shaped mineralizations lie at the base of large gypsum outcroppings. Black stars on a white field—the blazon of a crusader. The surface is delicate, and with each step there is a dry crushing of the ground; the desert floor is perceptibly altered. Everywhere the composition of the ground is distinct. Wind-driven, sun-broken particles of rock moved according to their size and weight create an even disposition about the surface. The desert is a topography of fine detail in trackless waste.

An outcrop on the horizon is the only distinct feature in the surrounding wilderness. As the distance narrows it is possible to make out, on top of the mound, a cow bellowing to the heavens. A stick is rammed between its jaws, the better to point its message. It is a desiccated carcass, hollow, eaten out by rodents, hairless. Set up beside the road and preserved by the aridity of the desert, this apparition dominates the landscape to the horizon. The effect is portentous, mythic. The carcass is increasingly defaced by travelers compelled to stop by its power. When I pass again later, the stick is broken and a dead snake has been cast over it and ignited. The dead cow brings forth gestural symbols that signify the fear of the desert. Through death it released a series of irrefutable images of mortality. The last time I see the carcass the destruction is complete; it is broken up and burned, and only a few of the major bones and a heap of ash remain. It has become a part of the fugitive mythology of the desert; the place is a landmark in time, identifying a place where travelers paused in the void.

The trapper of hawks

A man is sitting on a low rise in the desert. He is waiting at the side of the road with hawks tethered to stones by cords of palm fiber. The law of the desert requires the traveler to offer help. None is needed, and so I ask to make a picture. In the silence and heat of the midday desert he waits on, with no further interest in the circumstances of our meeting. He is going to Saudi Arabia to sell the birds for falconry. Raptors are fiercely independent and unwilling to be tamed and broken to jesses. The birds have not eaten since they were taken from the wild. All are in grave condition; one falls, flutters, dies as I work. There is no sound, the sun beats down, the trapper waits for deliverance, the birds die or will be sold. There is no pity; emotion is absent from the scene. I finish, put away the equipment, and continue south.

The desert is the ever-present fact at the periphery of Egyptian life. It is impossible to live in this country without an acute sense of the fragility of existence. The desert keeps the fertile valley within bounds while allowing green edens to spring forth from the geological depressions in its midst. These edens are the oases, which, in miraculous contrast to the surrounding wilderness, are so fertile that the contrast is even more sharply defined. The source of this abundance is ancient water from aquifers hidden deep beneath the desert. Men have sought refuge in these islands of the desert since ancient times. Oasis culture is vulnerable and the old ways continue through isolation, which is now being eroded by increased communication and access to the outside world.

The Omdah's garden

Behind the house of the Omdah, whose title indicates his position as head of the village, lies a walled garden where fruit and produce are grown. At dusk the shadows are long and the cool of the evening begins to descend with the setting sun. A table stands at the center of the garden. Bread is brought, and the Omdah's grandson gathers sweet lemons, still warm from the day; they are both substance and symbol of hospitality. The fruit, covered with the iridescent bloom of life, is laid before us; the Omdah bids us eat. The strange and exotic scent of the skin is redolent of the oases, the taste is unmistakable and indefinable; subtle and demonstrative, it lingers in the memory, an elusive taste, an indescribable lightness on the tongue.

An old, dignified man, the Omdah is renowned for his wisdom and hospitality; he is the arbiter in disputes involving such critical matters as distribution of water for irrigation. It is time for the evening irrigation as we sit in the garden, and water runs into each area of cultivation in turn; we are surrounded in the gathering darkness by shimmering water held back by slightly raised margins that define each section. The water is directed to a different compound with a few deft strokes of a mattock that closes one slender conduit and opens another. At sunset the muezzin calls the faithful to prayer from the mosque. We sit in the fast-falling night amidst apricot, pomegranate, and orange trees. Date palms with their long steely green fronds form a dark boundary to the garden. We take our leave and pass out into the night with people on their way home after work in the gardens behind the village. The diesel generator starts, light flickers into life. At eleven o'clock the true silence of the desert descends.

Qasr Farafra

As we walk up the wide approach to the village at dawn, light grazes the walls of the houses, showing the texture of sand and gypsum from which they are made. Building materials are readily at hand; all that is required to make a simple brick is to dig in the ground and add water. The naturally occurring gypsum makes a sufficient bond where rain is scarce. Roof beams, made from split trunks of date palms, are overlaid with palm fronds. The house is then stuccoed with the same mixture of sand and gypsum. Houses have a central courtyard; the plan is internalized, with no window to the outside. An offset inside the door opening onto the street prevents any view of the interior. The women's quarters are separate from those of the men, and the common family quarters are arranged around another courtyard in a series of rooms that are not interconnected. These photographs were permitted through the intercession of Mr. Ewes, the schoolteacher, who befriended me and took me with him to the homes of his pupils. An outsider from Alexandria, Mr. Ewes was able to understand and admire the quality of life in the small oasis; he spoke of how greatly it differed from the more strident urban life to which he had been accustomed prior to his posting to Farafra. He introduced us to our friends in the village, Mr. Badr, the painter, and Mr. Mohammed, the photographer.

The painter

In anticipation of his return from Mecca, a pilgrim's house is decorated with complex cartouches of Koranic inscriptions and scenes from the pilgrimage. There are also images alluding to a different, more ancient Egypt with roots in the pharaonic past. These show crouching and springing lions hunting gazelle, and hawks perched in trees, all painted in vivid colors and with a sure and vigorous hand. Mr. Badr is the goalkeeper from the village soccer team. A teacher of reading in the school, he teaches children during the day and adults in the evening. He is the painter. He chooses subjects that have been painted in Egypt since the time of the pharaohs, and his paintings have a hieratic aspect that is in perfect harmony with the walls of the houses he decorates. His evolution as a painter can be seen all around the village, for he has adorned many of the houses of returning pilgrims.

Mr. Badr is also a sculptor, and he uses materials in the same manner as the artisans who fabricated scenes of domestic life for the tombs of the pharaohs. He shapes wood into a gazelle, gessoes it and then finishes the sculpture with water-based pigments. He does not live in the past but rather thinks forward; he recognizes that the way of life in the oasis is changing faster now than it has in the preceding five millennia. To retain some vestiges of the old order he is assembling and classifying a collection of tools and implements and gathering specimens of the flora and fauna of the oasis.

At Sheikh Marzuq

In the shade of the trees, eight children sit in a circle reading; none stirs. We are observing a class composed of all the children in the village. The teacher has been sent by the government so that all might be able to read. We are taken to the house of the sheikh and offered tea. He gives us sweet dates gathered from the trees within a stone's throw of where we sit. In contrast, the fragrant mint tea has no sugar. One hundred paces away is the desert stretching for miles in every direction, beyond the endurance of man. The desert is all. We sit within sight of a pool of water surrounded by palm trees, the Western idea of an oasis. The simple school embodies the idea of a utopian enclave where time passes slowly. In this rigorous but essentially humane environment, autonomy has been achieved through isolation and the accumulated wisdom of an ancient way of life.

Near Qasr Farafra

It is late December, the time of the olive harvest. A short journey across the flat surrounding desert to a small outlying oasis used for the cultivation of a grove of trees. The family that has inherited the water rights to this carefully tended spring is engaged in the olive harvest. The modest network of hidden channels from the spring date back to Roman times and constitute one of the few antiquities of the region. Stripped palm fronds rattle among the sinuous boughs of the trees and the pattering of the falling fruit can be heard as the ground becomes covered with green and black olives. The children gather them into heaps separated by color. A fire is made from the tinder at hand. A few fronds of olive leaves are gathered and spread on the ground. On them are placed bread, lemons, and some of the first brine-cured olives of the season. A small teapot filled with water from the spring is set to boil. The tea is very strong, very sweet; bread is broken in the ritual of friendship.

Summer Ramadan

It is June; the weather is hot, but Allah is merciful and the heat is not intolerable. We are resting in the aromatic shade of Mr. Mohammed's garden. At midday each tree stands in its own shadow; this creates a symmetry that is strange to northern eyes. The irrigation channel, no wider than the span of a hand, runs nearby. A breeze passes through the trees for a moment, dispelling the midday calm. A donkey grazes in the distance. In the exhaustion and thirst of the afternoon the urge to seek oblivion in sleep is strong. Mr. Mohammed covers himself with a sheet in the shade of a grove of orange trees. The only sounds are the trickle of water in the channel and the donkey stamping with momentary unease in the stillness of the afternoon. The shadows lengthen and the sun sinks with what seems to be ineffable slowness toward the horizon.

As evening falls in the village all wait for the call to prayer from the mosque and the hour of the breaking of the fast. The call sounds, and after prayers the men seat themselves quickly at the table in the center of the courtyard. The first drink is the nectar of apricots. After the long, parched day the sulfurous water from the aquifer tastes sweet. Later, in the cool of the night, we sit on the enclosed roof of the painter's house listening to quiet conversation and speaking of the world beyond the oasis. One by one, the people slip away to sleep and make preparations for the meal before dawn, when the fast begins once more.

The mosque of Qajmas-al Ishaqi

The third time I go to this mosque, I have half an hour, time for one exposure only. The mosque is celebrated for the delicacy of its inlay and the quality of the woodwork in the minbar. The muezzin is preparing for the midday call to prayer. No one climbs the minaret any longer. The closest sense of what it must have been like to hear the beauty of a frail voice drifting across the silent city is to listen for the first and farthest call at dawn when it becomes possible to distinguish a black thread from a white. The muezzin is kneeling deep in prayer before the qibla; he rocks back and forth gently from time to time, and throughout the twenty minutes he makes no movement other than this. The shutter of the camera closes and the microphone is switched on with shattering effect; it is in discord with the deep contemplation that has preceded it.

The Northern Cemetery

Beneath the Muqattam hills, an escarpment to the east of the city from which the limestone for the pyramids was quarried, lies the cemetery of Cairo. The city of the dead stretches along the perimeter of the city, divided by the aqueduct that once carried water from the Nile to the Citadel. As the city of the living expands, the main thoroughfares in the cemetery are being taken over by the living; houses now stand where once there were tombs. The transition is incomplete as it is still in use as a cemetery. The tombs of the khalifs stand side by side with a truck repair shop, and spinners set up their wheels and stretch long skeins of silk in the alleyways between the tombs. It is quiet here, as the road is unpaved; there is little traffic in the city of the dead.

Standing at the axis of the cemetery is the mausoleum of Qaytbey, remarkable for its fine craftsmanship, beauty of design, and magnificent decoration. Once a place of retreat from the city, now the mausoleum is the crossroads of the cemetery with cafes and small shops clustered around. The view from the minaret encompasses the Citadel and the cemetery, and extends across the modern city to the pyramids in the far distance.

Egypt of the pharaohs

The history of pharaonic Egypt is written along the banks of the Nile in a sequence of ceremonial sites from Abu Simbel to Saqqara and Giza. Construction of the temple complexes was contingent upon being able to float building stone and completed sculptures from quarry to building site during the annual flood. Consequently all of the great centers of ancient Egypt stand just above the high water level of the Nile at the edge of the cultivated area.

Luxor and Thebes

The sun is already up as we cross the river on the first ferry of the morning, after passing through the quiet streets of Luxor. We approach the ferry landing on the banks of the river, banks of rich and fertile silt from old inundations. At this time of day, farmers from the west bank are the only passengers. The sense of continuity with ancient Egypt is vivid as they disembark with baskets of fowl and varied produce for the market in Luxor. Returning to the west bank, the ferry moves out across the limpid, slow-moving waters, past big riverboats, slumbering at the moorings beneath the big hotels. On the other side of the river away from the ferry point the countryside is still; farmers go about their work in the tranquility of the morning. The flood plain is covered with abundant crops of sugar cane and alfalfa. In the calm of the ancient landscape, the heat has not yet begun to gather its force.

The Colossi of Memnon, the two silent sentinels of the Theban necropolis, with their destroyed visages have the appearance of blind seers who have become mute through the accretion of years. At the edge of the cultivation the desert is kept at bay through the incessant labor of the farmer. The land beyond is immediately barren, and worn with use. It has none of the integrity of surface that can be seen in the more remote desert, altered only by natural forces.

Medinet Habu

The great funerary temple of Ramesses III, called Medinet Habu after the village that lies alongside it, looms large in the buildings of the west bank, one of the best preserved of the temples at Thebes. As the ancient religious center, it was the focus of ceremonial life on the west bank. Thebes is silent now with the guardians who watch over the temple resting in the deep shade of the porch. The sun beats down on the inner courtyard. In the still, dry air reflections from the massive walls intensify the heat. The sun sweeps slowly across the surface of the great pylon.

At the end of the day a guardian tells me to follow him. We walk around the great shaded bastion to the scene of Ramesses III hunting, carved on the reverse of the raked surface of the pylon. The fast-fading light illuminates the hunting scene, cut in low relief on the stone. It seems perfectly preserved, as sharply defined as on the day it was completed. The sun slides below the horizon as the exposure of the photograph goes forward. For a moment it seems as though life has returned to the king and his huntsmen. The illusion of reality in the carving of the scene—fish, ducks, and the dying wild bull struck through with the king's spear—gives a vivid glimpse into the life of the pharaoh. The light falls and the illusion passes with the declining day. The sites of Thebes recede into darkness to await the coming of a new dawn.

Saqqara

Imhotep, the first architect whose name has come down to us, constructed for the pharaoh Djoser the earliest structures built wholly in stone. In the late afternoon, the courtyard is deserted and the sun catches the engaged columns. They stand once more to suggest the splendor of this achievement. Standing before them at the end of the day leads one to reflect on temporality and the nature of continuity. At the edge of the desert beyond the life-giving waters of the Nile, the pyramids—these most ancient symbols of man's aspiration toward immortality—are surrounded by a mystical aura. The pyramids will remain as mute reminders long after all empires have ceased. In the words of an Arab proverb, ''Men fear time but time fears the pyramids.''

1   The Nile from Roda Island, Cairo.

2   The Western Desert, looking west from the edge of the Kharga depression.

3   Between the Kharga and Dakhla oases, Western Desert.

4   Trapper of hawks, Western Desert.

5   Cultivated oasis, Farafra depression, Western Desert.

6   Against the evil eye, Qasr Farafra, Western Desert.

7   Reception room, Qasr Farafra, Western Desert.

8 and 9   Courtyard, Qasr Farafra, Western Desert.

10 and 11   Bashendi, Dakhla depression, Western Desert.

12   Primary school, Sheikh Marzuq, Farafra depression, Western Desert.

13   The Omdah's garden, Qasr Farafra, Western Desert.

14   The Omdah's garden, Qasr Farafra, Western Desert.

15   Mihrab, primary school, El Qasr, Dakhla, Western Desert.

16 The old city from the minaret of the mosque of Sultan Barquq, looking south toward the minaret of al-Mansur Qala'un, Cairo.

17 The old city from the minaret of al-Azhar, looking south toward the Citadel and Bab Zuwayla, Cairo.

18 Mausoleum of Gani Bek al-Ashrafi and the mosques of al-Ashrafi Barsbay, Northern Cemetery, Cairo.

19   Mausoleum of Gani Bek al-Ashrafi, looking south from the mausoleum of Sultan Barquq, Northern Cemetery, Cairo.

20   Mosque and mausoleum of Sultan Qaytbay, Northern Cemetery, Cairo.

21   Mausoleum of Imam ash-Shafi'i, Southern Cemetery, Cairo.

22 Southeast corner of the mosque of Sultan Hasan, Cairo.

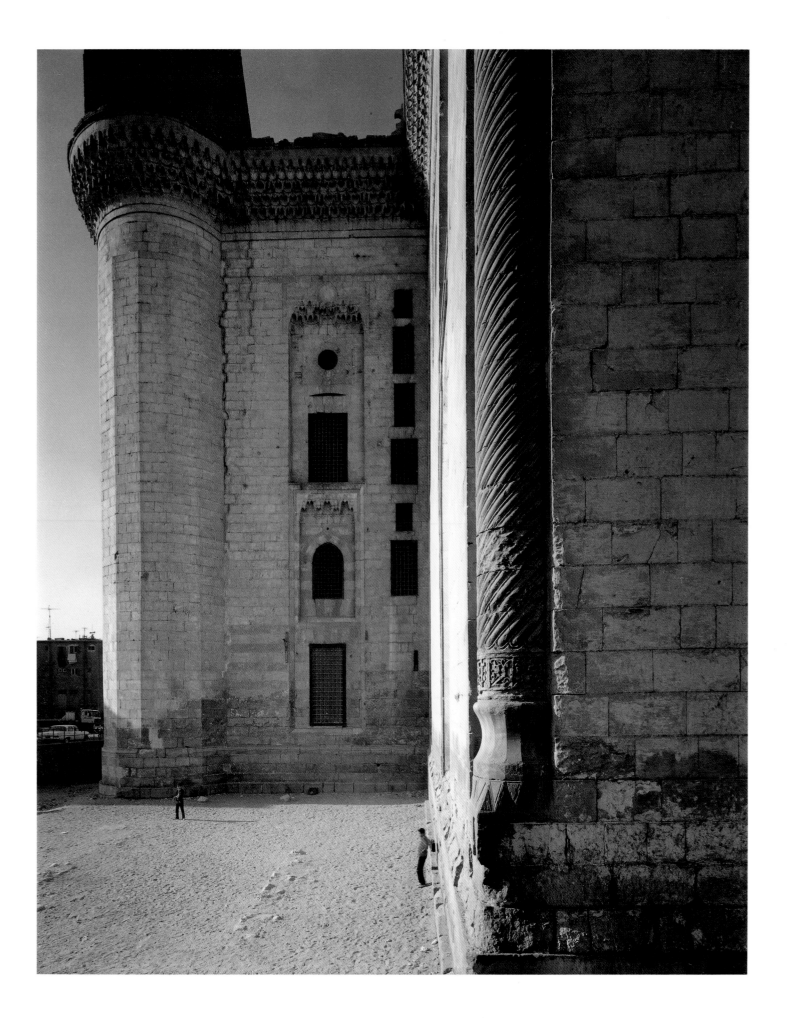

23   Mihrab in the mosque of Sultan Hasan, Cairo.

31   Minaret of the mosque of Amr ibn al-Asi from the potteries, Cairo.

35   Pyramid of Cheops from Pyramids Road, Giza.

40   Heraldic pillar of Tuthmosis III, Temple of Amun, Karnak.

42   Relief of Ramesses III, Medinet Habu, Thebes.

43   Detail of frieze, Medinet Habu, Thebes.

46   Pyramids of Cheops, Chephren, and Mycerinus, Giza.

47   The first masonry columns, Heb-sed court of Djoser, Saqqara.

48   Stepped pyramid of Djoser from the Nile floodplain, Saqqara.

49   Stepped pyramid of Djoser, Saqqara.

50   Stepped pyramid of Djoser, Saqqara.

51   Bent pyramid of Sneferu at Dashur, looking south from the walled enclosure, Saqqara.

The photographs in this book were made with an eight-by-ten-inch view camera
and were reproduced from contact prints made by the photographer.
Text set in Syntax by Finn Typographic, Inc., Stamford, with San Serif Bold by M & H, San Francisco.
Design by Eleanor Morris Caponigro.
Printed and bound by South China Printing Company, Hong Kong.
Library of Congress Cataloging-in-Publication Data
Pare, Richard.
    Egypt: reflections on continuity / Richard Pare.
       p.   cm.
      ISBN 0−943221−08−0
       1. Egypt−Civilization−Pictorial Works. I. Title.
  DT70.P37   1990
  962−dc20

Published by Timken Publishers, Inc.,
225 Lafayette Street, New York, NY 10012.